## HUMAN HABITATS

# HAIR

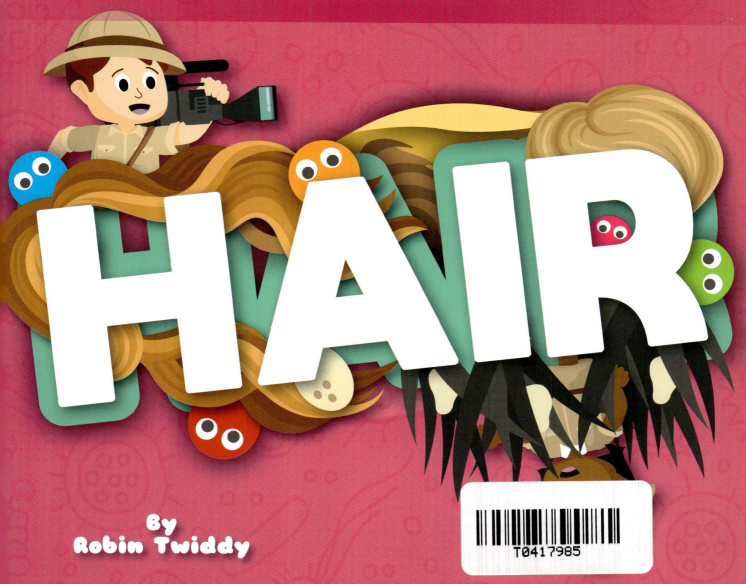

By
Robin Twiddy

Enslow
PUBLISHING

Published in 2022 by Enslow Publishing, LLC
101 W. 23rd Street, Suite 240,
New York, NY 10011

Copyright © 2022 Booklife Publishing
This edition published by arrangement with Booklife Publishing

All rights reserved.

No part of this book may be reproduced by any means without the written permission of the publisher.

Cataloging-in-Publication Data

Names: Twiddy, Robin.
Title: Hair / Robin Twiddy.
Description: New York : Enslow Publishing, 2022. | Series: Human habitats | Includes glossary and index.
Identifiers: ISBN 9781978523609 (pbk.) | ISBN 9781978523623 (library bound) | ISBN 9781978523616 (6 pack) | ISBN 9781978523630 (ebook)
Subjects: LCSH: Hair--Juvenile literature. | Human physiology--Juvenile literature.
Classification: LCC QP88.3 T95 2022 | DDC 573.5'8--dc23

Designer: Gareth Liddington
Editor: John Wood

Printed in the United States of America

CPSIA compliance information: Batch #CS22ENS: For further information contact Enslow Publishing, New York, New York at 1-800-542-2595

# TRICKY WORDS

Bacterium = singular (one bacterium)
Bacteria = plural (many bacteria)
Bacterial = to do with a bacterium or many bacteria

Fungus = singular (one fungus)
Fungi = plural (many fungi)
Fungal = to do with a fungus or many fungi

**Photo credits:**

Cover - GoodStudio, 4 - fun way illustration, ONYXprj, 9 - Henry Nine Graphics, 12 - Maquiladora, 14 - Roi and Roi, 22 - Creative Stall, peart.

Images are courtesy of Shutterstock.com. With thanks to Getty Images, Thinkstock Photo, and iStockphoto.

All facts, statistics, web addresses and URLs in this book were verified as valid and accurate at time of writing.
No responsibility for any changes to external websites or references can be accepted by either the author or publisher.

# CONTENTS

| | |
|---|---|
| Page 4 | Welcome to the Human Habitat |
| Page 6 | Hair, Hair Everywhere |
| Page 8 | Lice: Not Nice! |
| Page 10 | Scabies on the Scalp |
| Page 12 | Tricky Ticks |
| Page 14 | I Can't Flake This Feeling |
| Page 16 | I Believe in Bacteria |
| Page 18 | Ringworm – More like Wrongworm |
| Page 20 | Surprise Parasite! |
| Page 22 | Comb Here, Bye! |
| Page 24 | Glossary Index |

Words that look like <u>this</u> can be found in the glossary on page 24.

# WELCOME TO THE HUMAN HABITAT

Hi! I'm Mini Ventura. My cameraman, Dave, and I have been shrunk down so we can make a nature <u>documentary</u> all about the tiny things living in and on us. Follow us into the human <u>habitat</u> — a world within a world.

Face

Lungs

Mouth

Hair

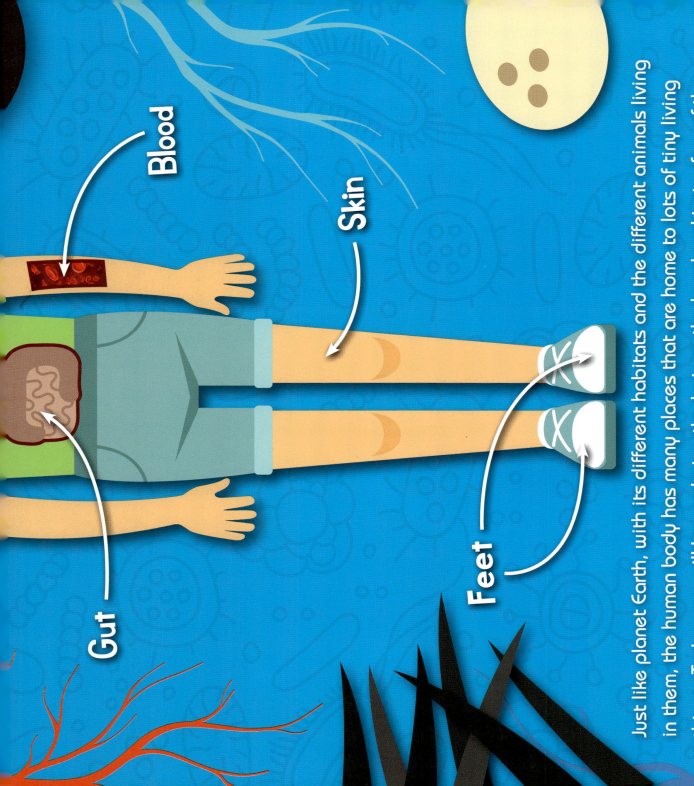

Just like planet Earth, with its different habitats and the different animals living in them, the human body has many places that are home to lots of tiny living things. Today, we will be exploring the hair on the head and just a few of the things living in it.

# HAIR, HAIR EVERYWHERE

This is the hair habitat. It is hot and thick like a jungle. It also has lots of life just like the jungle habitat.

Let's get in there and see what we can see!

There are lots of different things to see in the hair habitat. There are things that live here all the time and some things that are just visiting.

# LICE: NOT NICE!

Well, it looks like this hair forest has a case of lice — big ones, too. If you peer through the hair, you may see them.

I can tell that they are here because of all these eggs stuck to the hairs. They are sometimes called nits.

# SCABIES ON THE SCALP

Look at the bumps on the floor. They look like pimples, don't they? However, they are not normal pimples. They are signs that this <u>scalp</u> has scabies.

Scabies is caused by tiny <u>mites</u> that burrow under the skin.

10

# TRICKY TICKS

Ticks are <u>related</u> to mites. Just like mites, they are bloodsuckers who will bury their heads into the host's skin and drink. Their bodies swell up when they feed.

> I saw a tick bite back there. That means there must be one hiding around here somewhere.

# I CAN'T FLAKE THIS FEELING

Ah, look, can you see this? It is like snow on the ground. But that is not snow. That is dandruff. Dandruff is loose flakes of skin from the scalp.

# I BELIEVE IN BACTERIA

There are lots of things living high up in the hair jungle, but we are now going to look at the scalp floor. Here we can find a lot of different bacteria.

Wow, look, that is an *E. coli*, and over there is an *S. epidermidis*. I love bacteria!

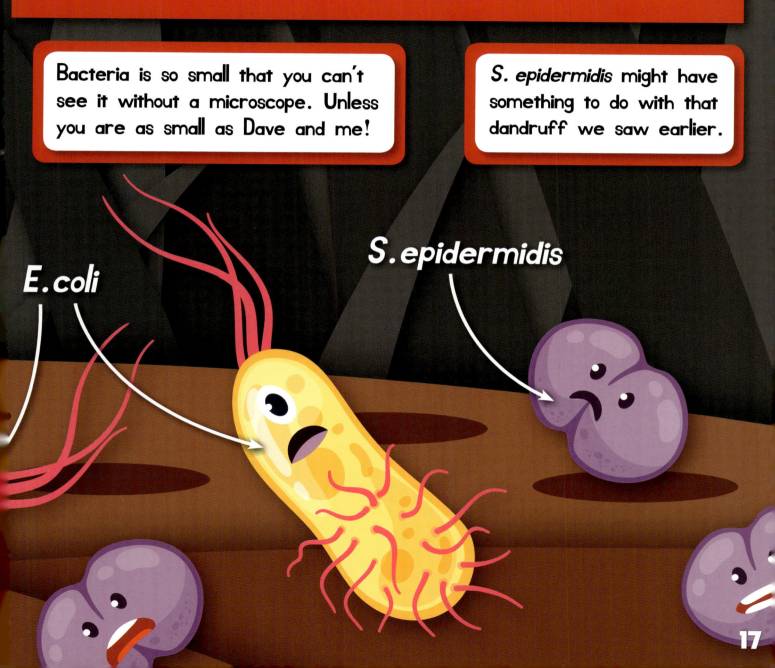

# RINGWORM - MORE LIKE WRONGWORM

And here, in this clearing, we find a mysterious red ring on the scalp. It seems that most of the hair has fallen out here.

Ringworm is caused by the same type of fungi as athlete's foot.

# SURPRISE PARASITE!

Aha! Here we have a rare parasite. It is the human botfly, which is mostly found in Central and South America. The human botfly maggot burrows into the skin of a host.

Dave, I have found something better than a worm over here. It's a maggot!

# COMB HERE, BYE!

Who knew that there was so much life on the human head? All this thick hair is the perfect place for tiny things to hide.

# GLOSSARY

| | |
|---|---|
| bacteria | tiny living things, too small to see, that can cause diseases |
| documentary | a film that looks at real facts and events |
| fungus | a living thing that often looks like a plant but has no flowers |
| habitat | the natural home in which animals, plants, and other living things live |
| mites | tiny arachnids of the same family as spiders |
| parasite | a creature that lives on or in another creature |
| rare | uncommon, hard to find |
| related | connected or part of the same group |
| scalp | the skin that covers the top of the head |

# INDEX

bacteria 16–17
bites 12
blood 5, 9, 12
dandruff 14–15, 17
eggs 8, 11
fungi 15, 18–19
hair 4–9, 13, 16–18, 22–23

lice 8–9, 23
maggots 20–21
mites 10–12
parasites 20–21
pimples 10
scalp 10–11, 14–18
yeast 15

24